FINANCIAL LITERACY

EARNING, SAVING, AND INVESTING

By Sue Bradford Edwards

CONTENT CONSULTANT
Dr. Linda Simpson, PhD, CFCS, CPFFE
Professor
Eastern Illinois University

Essential Library

An Imprint of Abdo Publishing | abdobooks.com

ABDOBOOKS.COM

Published by Abdo Publishing, a division of ABDO, PO Box 398166, Minneapolis, Minnesota 55439. Copyright © 2020 by Abdo Consulting Group, Inc. International copyrights reserved in all countries. No part of this book may be reproduced in any form without written permission from the publisher. Essential Library™ is a trademark and logo of Abdo Publishing.

Printed in the United States of America, North Mankato, Minnesota.
022019
092019

THIS BOOK CONTAINS
RECYCLED MATERIALS

Cover Photo: Mikhail Mishchenko/Shutterstock Images
Interior Photos: Shutterstock Images, 5, 10, 21, 43, 49; iStockphoto, 15, 30, 32, 37, 59, 87, 89, 90, 94; Aigars Reinholds/Shutterstock Images, 18; Rich Legg/iStockphoto, 23; Steve Debenport/iStockphoto, 27; Red Line Editorial, 40, 62, 93; Global Stock/iStockphoto, 47; ESB Professional/Shutterstock Images, 57; Robert D. Barnes/Moment Open/Getty Images, 67; Wave Break Media/iStockphoto, 72; Montri Nipitvittaya/Shutterstock Images, 77; Alison Buck/TheWrap/Getty Images Entertainment/Getty Images, 80; Carlos Osorio/AP Images, 83; David Pereiras/Shutterstock Images, 97

Editor: Alyssa Krekelberg
Series Designer: Colleen McLaren

LIBRARY OF CONGRESS CONTROL NUMBER: 2018965871

PUBLISHER'S CATALOGING-IN-PUBLICATION DATA

Names: Edwards, Sue Bradford, author.
Title: Earning, saving, and investing / by Sue Bradford Edwards
Description: Minneapolis, Minnesota : Abdo Publishing, 2020 | Series: Financial
    literacy | Includes online resources and index.
Identifiers: ISBN 9781532119118 (lib. bdg.) | ISBN 9781532173295 (ebook)
Subjects: LCSH: Saving and investment--Juvenile literature. | Capital
    accumulation--Juvenile literature. | Accumulated earnings--Juvenile
    literature. | Money funds--Juvenile literature. | Personal budgets--
    Juvenile literature.
Classification: DDC 332.024--dc23

So all readers may use the worksheets, please complete the exercises in your own notebook.

CONTENTS

CHAPTER ONE

MONEY MATTERS

Makayla pulled into the driveway, set the parking brake, and then waved at her best friend, Felicity, who sat waiting for her on the front porch. As Makayla and her father climbed out of the car, she told Felicity that her car loan had been approved but that now she felt like she was broke.

Felicity was happy for her friend but also a bit jealous. Felicity knew that when she started college in a few months she would be riding the bus instead of driving a car. Both she and Makayla had jobs, but Felicity hadn't been able to get a car loan. She asked her friend how she got approved for the loan.

Makayla was proud of her new car and the fact that she had worked hard to get it. She explained to Felicity that she had put aside 10 to 15 percent of her paycheck each week, as well as most of the tips she got as a server. Makayla had also opened a bank account in order to save money where she wouldn't

Buying a car is a big purchase. People should do their research and not make any quick decisions.

TAKING OUT A LOAN

Someone who wants to buy a car but hasn't saved the necessary money can take out a car loan. This person usually makes a small down payment, which pays off part of the car, and borrows the remaining money from a bank or finance company. Each month, he or she will make a car payment, which pays off a small part of the loan. Generally, the loan will last three to five years until the car is paid off. Car loans for six to seven years are available, but paying interest for this long often results in repaying more than the car is worth. In addition to taking out loans to buy cars, people also use loans to buy other high-cost items such as a college education or a house.

spend it. Having a big enough down payment made it easier for Makayla to get a loan.

Felicity nodded along as her friend talked. Then, she asked Makayla to explain in detail how she was able to save her money.

LEARNING ABOUT MONEY

Many young adults don't think about money until they want to buy something they can't afford. Part of the reason is that if they get a job while they are in high school, they might feel as though they have a lot of money. This is because the majority of teens live with their parents or guardians and probably don't have to pay for expenses such as rent, groceries, or utilities.

With so many of their expenses already paid, most adolescents can use their earnings as discretionary income, which is income that can be spent on whatever they want. Sometimes they buy small things such as beverages and snacks that don't cost much. These teens may also be making mid-range purchases on things such as clothing and movie tickets. But when they want to buy something big, such as an expensive phone or a car, they cannot afford it. That's because they've spent most of their money on small to mid-range purchases.

To avoid these situations, it is important for young people to educate themselves about money and how

DISCRETIONARY INCOME

Once a person has paid for all of his or her necessities, including housing, food, transportation, and clothing, the remaining money is called discretionary income. Discretionary income is money that can be spent at the person's discretion, meaning the person can spend it freely on whatever he or she wants. The person can spend it on something fun, such as going to a concert, or on a luxury, such as a cruise, but this money doesn't have to be spent. It can also be saved or invested and allowed to grow.

BUILDING A CREDIT HISTORY

A credit history is a person's individual history of paying bills. A good credit history is necessary to get a credit card or a loan. The first step in building a good credit history is to get and hold a job, because working at the same job over time shows potential creditors that a person is reliable. The second step is to open a checking account, which is a bank account that can be used to pay bills. Keeping more money in this account than is paid out shows the person is responsible and knows how to handle money. With this checking account in place, the person can then get a credit card from the bank. A credit card allows a person to charge items to the card and then pay off his or her credit card each month. This builds an even stronger history. Employment, a checking account, and a credit card will help establish the history needed to get a loan or rent an apartment.

to handle it. Not only do they need to know how to earn money, they need to understand the concept of saving, or putting money aside, so that they don't run out of it and can make larger purchases, such as paying for college or a car. In addition, they need to learn about investment, which is how to use money to make more money.

Whether people read articles and books or talk to professionals who know about the finance industry, the topic of money can get confusing fast. Interest can be simple or compound, variable or fixed, and money can go into savings accounts, checking accounts, and even money market accounts. Finance professionals even offer differing advice. For example, one finance professional might recommend low-risk investments, while another might advise higher-risk investments.

Because of the confusion factor and contradictory advice, many people give up without learning all that's necessary to smartly earn, save, and spend their money. Sometimes, they have enough money to buy whatever they need and want. But other times, they don't—especially when they want to make a major purchase. It is important for young people to learn how to save and manage money before they have to pay all of their own bills.

PERSONAL MONEY MANAGEMENT

Learning about earning, saving, and investing, as well as responsible spending, can lead to financial security. Financially secure people are not constantly worried about money and whether they will be able to pay their bills. Financially secure people live in sharp contrast with people who cannot or do not pay their bills on time, which leads to having to pay the bill plus an additional fee. These late fees, missed payment fees,

and penalties add up, and soon people sink deeper into debt.

A person who knows how to handle his or her personal finances is more likely to be able to buy the things he or she wants. Depending on what matters to this person, this can mean having the money to travel or attend sporting events. It can also mean being able to pay for a luxury car or help pay for college tuition. Being able to do these things all begins with understanding how a person can earn money, save money, and make investments.

Some high schools offer financial literacy classes.

HOW DO YOU HANDLE MONEY?

Answering these questions can reveal a person's money style.

1. You go on a weeklong school trip and only have cash to pay for food. What scenario do you think you would find yourself in?

    a. You run out of money before the last meal and have to borrow from a friend.

    b. You know exactly how much you can spend on each meal, and even end up not spending it all.

2. The money for the school fund-raiser is due tomorrow. Where is it?

    a. You spend all evening looking around your room to find where you dropped it.

    b. You have it in the envelope on your dresser.

3. When the cashier tells you the snacks for you and your friends will be $11.50, what do you do?

    a. You have to figure out what to put back. You didn't know what the total would be and only have $10.

b. You hand the cashier the $10 bill your guardian gave you and the $5 you had from your allowance. You knew $10 wouldn't be quite enough.

4. When your teacher asks for your field trip money, what do you do?

a. Dig through your backpack. You know it is in there somewhere.

b. Pull the money out of your wallet.

5. Your guardian gave you $20 to pay for a new pair of swim goggles. When you get home, he asks for the change.

a. What change? You already spent it.

b. You hand him the change and the receipt.

If three or more of your answers were "a," then you probably don't keep good track of your money. You expect there to always be more when you need it. You may not value it or the things it can buy. If three or more of your answers were "b," then you are probably careful with money. You think about what you spend and how far the money needs to go.

CHAPTER TWO

GETTING A JOB

The first step for young people who want to learn how to save and invest money is to keep track of their income. Even before their first job, some teens get money for birthdays and holidays, and some get an allowance. Some guardians require their teen to pay for certain things, such as clothing or school expenses, so these teens learn to put part of their money aside to pay for future expenses. That's how good money habits begin.

If a teen gets an allowance, one problem is that the allowance is limited. A teen who wants to earn more might offer to do additional chores for an increase in allowance. If teens have handled money well, they can also point out that they can be trusted with more. However, there could be a limit to how much allowance teens get. Teens can likely earn more by doing chores for neighbors and family members. If they are

Getting a job can help people develop a good work ethic.

14

industrious enough and pull in enough customers, it can turn into a job.

UNEXPECTED INCOME

To some people, gift cards and cash received for birthdays or holidays may seem like free money, but it is still important to manage them wisely. Andrea Woroch is a consumer adviser who works for the internet-marketing company Kinoli. "Don't spend just to spend," Woroch says.[1] Instead, she advises people to ask themselves a question when deciding to buy something: do I really want or need this? This question is especially important if the item costs more than the gift card is worth, because the purchase will require out-of-pocket expenses. Also, instead of spending cash as it comes in, people can always save it and wait to use it on a large purchase.

SELF-EMPLOYED

When someone is self-employed, that person works for himself or herself and often provides a service for other people. If a person is self-employed, he should research how to properly report his income to the government. He should also look into other legal requirements that are necessary when building a business.

Some of the easiest jobs for teens to find are self-employed service jobs, such as childcare, mowing lawns, cleaning gutters,

MOZIAH "MO" BRIDGES

Moziah "Mo" Bridges always had a strong sense of fashion—he was known to wear three-piece suits to the playground. But even at nine years old, he didn't like the boring bow ties he could find at stores in his hometown of Memphis, Tennessee. His grandmother, a former seamstress, taught him to sew, which led to him, his grandmother, and his mother making and selling bow ties. He appeared on *Shark Tank* in 2014. In this reality TV show, entrepreneurs present their ideas to five investors, the sharks. They hope the sharks will offer to invest the money that will move their business plans forward. Moziah's appearance on the show resulted in investor Daymond John mentoring the young entrepreneur. "One of the most important things he's taught me was to always be true to my company," said Moziah.[2] Staying true means sometimes turning down offers from people who want to work with Mo's Bows and only accepting the offers that mesh with his goals for fashion and quality. At 16 years old, he signed a seven-figure offer to create ties for every team in the National Basketball Association.

walking dogs, and running errands. Teens who like to work with their hands can do household repairs or make items. Teens with a knack for sales can even turn a small side business, such as making bow ties, into a home-based business and sell their product. That's what entrepreneur Moziah "Mo" Bridges did, eventually creating a company called Mo's Bows that

makes fashionable bow ties and pocket squares. Entrepreneurs organize and operate businesses.

Being self-employed isn't for everyone. People have to be incredibly focused to be able to get a job done when they could be sleeping in, watching television, or doing something with family and friends. It can be especially difficult for a teen because parents, guardians, and other relatives have to be willing to let self-employed teens manage their own time without trying to direct their activities. Part of this work time will have to be spent finding people who need the services these teens provide.

Some jobs, such as mowing lawns, can be fairly easy to get. That's because during the spring and summer, grass needs to be cut, and not everyone wants to do this tiring job or has the time to do it. But to do this particular job, a teen has to be able to handle the physical demands and have access to a lawn mower. Word of mouth can be a good way to find clients when satisfied customers share the teen's contact information with other people who need help.

In addition to finding customers, anyone who works for themselves needs to be ready to deal with customers. To start, this means negotiating exactly

Being self-employed can be hard work, but it can also be rewarding.

what a job includes. If a customer asks a teen for more work, the teen needs to be prepared to ask for more money. This will mean knowing how much to charge for the job and how much to add to this fee for extra work. After the job is completed, the teen will need to invite feedback and be able to deal with constructive criticism. Sometimes, this will involve how a customer wants a job done, with precise instructions for his or her yard or a specific bedtime routine for the babysitter to follow. Other times, it may involve an unhappy customer, and the teen will have to try to make things right. Customer satisfaction is key to running a successful business. This could include redoing the job to achieve customer satisfaction or reviewing what the customer wants in the future. Teens who can handle this may enjoy working for themselves, but it will take time to find enough clients to have a steady paycheck—especially if a teen is doing a job with a friend and splitting the income.

WORKING FOR WAGES

Not all teens work for themselves. Many choose to work for local businesses. A regular weekly schedule— such as at a grocery store, fast-food restaurant, or movie theater—can guarantee a reliable check.

Working with customers can be a positive experience for some teens.

APPLICATION ANXIETY

Job applications can be intimidating, but most request the same things, starting with the applicant's personal data: name, address, and contact information. Job applications also ask applicants for past employment history. This includes previous job titles, start and end dates on the jobs, the full name of each company, and the companies' addresses and phone numbers. References are always requested and should include names of people who will vouch for the applicant. Each reference should list first and last name, title, organization, address, and phone number. Former bosses are excellent references, but other people, such as coaches, scout leaders, and teachers, are also able to address personal attributes such as character, motivation, and ethics.

This can be important for a teen who is saving up money for college or to purchase an expensive item, such as a car.

Working for a local business is also a good choice for an extrovert who wants to work with people. For someone like this, working at a retail store or local swimming pool can be a good choice. The activity level and the opportunities to interact with coworkers and customers can create a good working environment for extroverts.

Teens who want to work for someone else should monitor their social media posts.

Some teens like working in the summer.

Potential employers often check an applicant's feed. A teen who posts photos of inappropriate behavior or offensive content may find it hard to get a job.

The choice between being self-employed and working for someone else is a decision that everyone needs to make for themselves. The decision also needs to be reviewed periodically as different employment opportunities arise. Another choice job seekers must make is whether to work year round or seasonally.

SEASONAL WORK

Some jobs are seasonal, or available only at certain times of the year. These include summer jobs such as mowing lawns or lifeguarding at pools. They also can include retail jobs when stores bring in extra people during the busy holiday season. In addition, home-and-garden stores hire more employees during the summer months. Resorts, hotels, and theme parks hire people during peak vacation seasons. People can also get seasonal jobs in agricultural work.

With seasonal jobs, employers usually need people to start work immediately. They hire a lot of people and they hire them fast, which means applicants aren't waiting around for weeks after turning in a job application. Part of the reason for this quick hiring process is that these jobs are considered unskilled, and seasonal employees may not make much money per hour. However, there are opportunities for a lot of hours for as long as the job lasts.

Seasonal jobs are a good way for teens to gain work experience that could lead to other positions with the same company. For example, someone who does well watering spring plants at a home-and-garden center may be offered a position in another department when the seasonal job ends.

CHOOSING A JOB

Some teens aren't sure what kind of job they should take. Doing a cost-benefit analysis can be helpful to see which job is the best choice.

	JOB ONE	JOB TWO
How much does the job pay?		
Is there an unpaid training period?		
Are uniforms or other clothing required? Who is responsible for the initial purchase and care of the uniform?		
Are special tools required? Who is responsible for the purchase?		
Calculate travel. How far do you need to travel to get to each job? Does the job require you to have a car?		
Is the job that pays the best hourly wage still the best option when other expenses, such as travel and special tools, are taken into consideration?		

Job choice: _____

CHAPTER THREE

TAKE-HOME PAY

One of the most important lessons new employees have to learn is how much money they will get to take home. Some people assume that if they work 15 hours a week for $10 an hour, they will get to take home $150. That figure is the person's gross pay, which is calculated by multiplying the number of hours worked times the hourly wage or rate of pay. However, gross pay is not take-home pay.

Take-home pay, also known as net income, is the gross pay minus a variety of deductions. Deductions are various things that are subtracted from a person's paycheck and can include company benefits such as health insurance, payments related to the Federal Insurance Contributions Act (FICA), and federal and state taxes. The amount deducted varies from person to person depending, in part, on the information provided on his or her Employee's Withholding Allowance Certificate, or W-4 form.

Working hard and earning money can be a rewarding experience for teens.

BENEFITS

Benefits are programs provided by an employer and designed to benefit the employee. The most common benefit is health insurance, but other health-related benefits can include health and wellness programs such as nutrition programs, access to fitness facilities, and sick days. Sick days are a set number of paid days that an employee can take off work due to illness. Other benefits include paid vacation days, childcare, eldercare, moving expenses, and tuition reimbursement. Good benefits can make it worthwhile to stay with a job that may not pay as well as another job. These benefits can be considered tax-free additions to the overall salary received. One employer may offer a high salary with no benefits, while another employer will offer a lesser salary with benefits. Choosing to take a job should not be based on income alone.

PAYING TAXES

All new employees are required to complete a W-4 form. Personal information that is requested on this form includes a person's name, address, marital status, and number of children.

The information found on the W-4 form can be changed or updated at any time. This is important, because the form helps determine how much money in taxes is withheld from the gross pay. These may include federal, state, and city taxes. All workers pay federal income taxes, but some states and cities do not tax incomes. These income taxes are pooled together and are used to pay for government expenses. Federal withholding taxes go to the federal government, state withholding taxes go to the state government, and any city taxes go to the city government.

The US tax system is a progressive income tax system, which means that people who make more money pay a higher percentage of their income in taxes. Taxes paid are also based on the number of exemptions people claim. Each exemption represents a person supported by this income. In addition to the exemption for themselves, older people may have an exemption for a spouse or children. As a result, the person pays less in taxes than someone who makes the same amount of money but has no deductions other than himself or herself.

TAXES MATTER

People often view taxes in a negative light, as it may be difficult to see the essential services that taxes support. People may work to pay as little in taxes as possible despite the fact that taxes pay for many critical services. Federal taxes pay for the military, important government departments, and health insurance programs. Taxes also pay for food stamps, public education, and the construction and repair of roads and bridges.

At the beginning of each year, Americans file their tax returns. This form shows not only how much income they made but how much they paid in taxes. They get the totals, both earnings and taxes paid, from a form called a W-2. Employers give all their employees W-2 forms. The W-2 lists income as well as state and federal taxes.

When Americans file this tax paperwork, they calculate how much money they owe the government in taxes that year. If the taxes withheld from their paychecks add up to more than they owe, they get money back from the government, which is called a refund. Those who did not pay enough in taxes must send in a check to pay the difference. Because the amount of tax a person owes is based on total income for the year, a teen who doesn't earn a lot, such as a teen who only works in the summer, may get much of the tax money he or she paid back as a refund.

FICA AND BENEFITS

More common deductions are included in FICA, a set of two taxes that go into separate federal funds. The first is Social Security, which deducts 6.2 percent of the total pay from a person's paycheck. Employers

The US Internal Revenue Service (IRS) suggests that people keep copies of their tax returns.

Even after retiring, people should calculate how much money they need to pay for their expenses.

also pay 6.2 percent of each employee's check to Social Security.[1] In 2018, the Social Security fund paid benefits to 63 million Americans.[2] People who receive benefits include retired workers and disabled workers and their spouses. The amount of money someone receives isn't meant to fully support the person but simply to improve the person's standard of living. In mid-2017, the average payment was $1,391 per month for a retired worker, $1,172 per month for a disabled worker, and $2,278 for a married disabled worker.[3]

The second portion of FICA is 1.45 percent of a person's paycheck and pays for Medicare, a national health insurance program. Again, the employer pays another 1.45 percent of the person's paycheck into the fund.[4] Insurance through Medicare is available to people over age 65, those who are dying of kidney failure, and some younger people with specific health problems.

These aren't the only deductions, as many employees have money withheld from their paychecks to pay for things such as health insurance and retirement funding. As a benefit for their full-time workers, many employers negotiate with an insurance

HEALTH INSURANCE

Health insurance helps a person pay for a wide variety of medical expenses including periodic wellness checkups, vaccinations, and screenings—such as breast exams—that are designed to keep people healthy. Health insurance also helps pay for expenses when someone is sick or injured. These can include emergency room fees, hospital stays, physical therapy following surgery or an injury, allergy treatments, mental health care, and prescription medications. Typically, the more a health insurance policy covers, the more expensive it is.

UNIONS: NEGOTIATING AS A GROUP

A union is an organization of workers that labors together to ensure decent work conditions and benefits. Unions may negotiate salaries, hours worked per day or week, or working conditions. When a union is concerned that conditions for workers are unsafe, it approaches the business owners or managers and demands change. If an agreement can't be reached between the union and the corporation, the result may be a strike. This means that, as a group, employees refuse to work for this employer until changes are made. In the United States, there are unions for teachers, carpenters, electrical workers, steelworkers, and more. Not all employees belong to unions, but those who work in an industry with a union may be required to join and pay union dues to support the organization.

company for a company-wide health insurance program. The employer pays part of the expense and so does the employee, with the employee's share being deducted from his or her paycheck. The amount deducted will depend on the deal negotiated by the employer and may also depend on how many people are being insured. Sometimes, people only insure themselves, but they may also insure a spouse and children. Other possible paycheck deductions include union dues, savings programs, and fees to pay for lunch in the company cafeteria or parking in a parking garage.

1040 FORM

At the beginning of the year, most Americans file their income taxes. While people who make less than $10,400 do not have to file, taxes already deducted from their paychecks will not be returned unless they do file.[5] The most standard tax return form is the 1040. Below is the necessary information required on the form. Do you have the information you need to fill out this form? Check off each box when you have the information.

☐ **Personal information.** The top of the form includes personal information such as name and address. You will need to know your Social Security number.

☐ **Income.** Your income is on the W-2 form provided by your employer. If this didn't come in the mail, let your employer know.

☐ **Taxes.** You will need to fill in the amount of federal income taxes withheld. The amount can be found on your W-2.

☐ **Refund.** If you are getting a refund, you can include your bank's routing number and have the money deposited directly into your account. If you aren't sure what the routing number is, call your bank.

CHAPTER FOUR

WAYS TO SAVE

n addition to paying attention to how much they earn, financially savvy people also learn how to save. The first step in saving is for people to learn how to budget or estimate their income and expenses. To create a budget, a person lists income and expenses for the month. By studying the budget at the end of the month, it becomes obvious how much money is being spent in a particular area, such as concession-stand snacks at school sporting events, online music, essential items for a school uniform, or transportation costs.

Creating a budget lets people see if they aren't saving any money because they are spending too much. They may not be able to cut what they spend on essentials, such as school items, but they can limit what they spend at the concession stand or on music. This might mean going to each game knowing that if they only spend $10 at the concession stand, they

Looking over weekly expenses and earnings can help people manage their money.

can start saving money. Sometimes money can be saved by cutting out one category completely, such as by making coffee instead of visiting the coffee shop, or checking out movies from the library rather than subscribing to a streaming video service. But these situations aren't the only ways to save.

BUDGET REBOOT AND TRADE-OFFS

Budgeting is a good habit to form, but budgets should be reviewed every few months. Increased income might mean a bit more can be saved. A new expense might mean deciding something else can no longer be purchased at that time. Deciding where and when to spend money can mean making a trade-off, or spending on one thing instead of another. Reviewing a budget is also a good time to make sure debts are not accumulating and to review savings goals— especially if a major expense, such as buying items for a dorm room, is coming up in the next year.

BANK ACCOUNTS

One of the best ways to save is to put money in the bank. Money in a bank account is still available for use, but unlike having cash on hand, it takes some effort to get to it. Many people put money into a checking account, which is primarily used for paying bills and fees for services. When a person wants to make a payment on a car, he or she can fill out and mail a check to the loan

PAY YOURSELF FIRST

It is easy for people to say they are going to save but never get around to doing it. This is why financial experts such as David Blaylock, a former certified financial planner at LearnVest Planning Services, say you should pay yourself first. "Paying yourself first means saving before you do anything else," Blaylock says. "Try and set aside a certain portion of your income the day you get paid. . . . Most people wait and only save what's left over—that's paying yourself last."[1]

People who pay themselves first and think about the money they spend don't tend to be surprised when bills arrive and need to be paid. When there are unplanned, emergency expenses, saving first means these bills can often be paid without taking all of someone's savings. Learning to save first can be a difficult habit to form, so experts recommend automating savings as much as possible. For example, when a person has his or her paycheck deposited directly into a bank account, the deposit can often be set up to put a portion automatically into a separate savings account.

company. Although checks are still sometimes written out by hand, more and more often the bill is paid online, directly from a bank account.

A savings account, as the name suggests, is better for savings. A person cannot directly spend this money using a check or debit card. The person who owns the account has to go to the bank to withdraw money from a savings account. He or she may also be able to transfer the money to a checking account, but overall,

SAVINGS RATES, 2018[2]

Although saving is important for financial security, some Americans admit that they don't save the recommended 10 percent of their income.

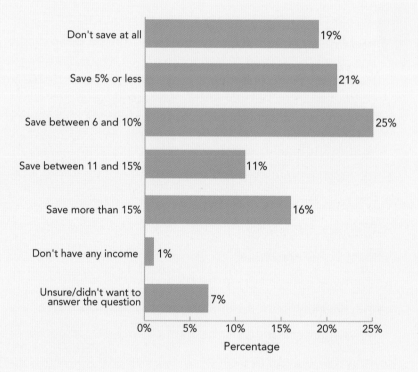

Don't save at all — 19%
Save 5% or less — 21%
Save between 6 and 10% — 25%
Save between 11 and 15% — 11%
Save more than 15% — 16%
Don't have any income — 1%
Unsure/didn't want to answer the question — 7%

Percentage

the money is harder to access. This makes it easier to save, and savings accounts pay an interest rate, which determines the money the bank pays people to borrow their money. Interest rates vary, but the best accounts can have a rate of around 2 percent a year.[3]

CERTIFICATES OF DEPOSIT

A savings account earns some interest, but a Certificate of Deposit (CD) earns more. When people put their money into a CD, they are agreeing to leave it in the bank for a set period of time ranging from several months to several years. The money is on loan to the bank, which then uses it to loan to other people who need money, perhaps to buy a car or a house.

In exchange for leaving the money in the bank for a set period of time, people who took out the CD will be paid more interest than they

FORMING A SAVINGS HABIT

Experts advise people who want to learn to save money to put some money aside every day. This will help people to create a savings habit. According to a study by Phillippa Lally, a health psychology researcher at University College London, it takes weeks for someone to develop a habit. This might mean they are developing a good habit, like saving money, or dropping a bad habit, like overspending.

would make from a savings account. The longer the money is left in the CD, the better the interest rate, which might be 2.4 percent for five years but only 1 percent for six months.[4] A CD is a low-risk way to use money to make money. When the CD matures, or reaches the date when it can be cashed in, the investor gets the original money and the interest. The downside is that if people take the money back before the CD matures, they have to pay a penalty.

SAVINGS BONDS

Another way to save money is with a savings bond. A savings bond is a promissory note that states that after a certain date, the US Department of the Treasury will pay the person who has the note a set amount of money. Currently, there are two types of bonds that people can buy: series EE bonds and series I bonds.

When someone buys a series EE bond, the person pays one-half of the face value, meaning that for a $50 bond, the person pays $25. A bond earns interest every month, but the person does not get the interest until he or she turns in the bond for cash. The person has to wait at least 12 months and then gets 12 months of interest in addition to the investment. Series EE

Some people use their savings bonds to help pay for college.

bonds reach their face value in 20 years and will continue to earn interest for 30 years.

When someone buys a series I bond, he or she pays the face value of the bond, meaning he or she pays $50 for a $50 bond. The interest paid on I bonds fluctuates somewhat based on inflation.

When someone buys bonds, the person has to wait at least five years to cash them in without penalty. The Bureau of Public Debt, part of the US Department of the Treasury, announces the interest rate on bonds in May and November of each year. Bonds are low-risk investments that are guaranteed to pay off the money invested plus interest.

CREATING A BUDGET

The following outline can be used to create a basic budget each month. Once you've calculated your monthly income and expenses, determine whether you have a surplus or deficit of money by subtracting your expenses from your income.

MONTH/YEAR:

INCOME

- Paycheck(s):
- Gift(s):
- Allowance:
- Other:

TOTAL: _____

EXPENSES

- School:
- Food:
- Transportation (car payment, fuel, maintenance/ upkeep):
- Clothing:
- Entertainment:
- Other:

TOTAL: _____

CHAPTER FIVE

INTEREST

When people take out a loan, they pay interest on the money they have borrowed. When people save money in a bank account, the bank pays them interest on the money. In short, interest is a percentage of a certain amount of money. It can be confusing because the same term is used whether it is interest on savings or interest on a loan.

When someone borrows money, the interest the person pays is a fee paid to the bank for providing the loan. The amount paid is a percentage of the loan amount. For example, if someone borrowed $10,000 to buy a car and had five years to pay the loan back, the person would also have to pay interest. In 2018, interest rates on car loans usually ranged from 3 percent to 10 percent per year.[1] These are annual percentage rates (APRs).

When someone saves or invests money, interest is the income the person receives. It is the fee paid by

People take out loans for a variety of reasons. One reason is to purchase a house.

the bank or credit union for the privilege of holding and using this person's money. Some people reason that any interest is better than no interest. The higher the interest rate, the more income they will make.

One way to compare investments is to use the Rule of 72. This method estimates the number of years needed to double an investment at a certain compound interest rate. For example, if someone is looking at a CD with 8 percent compound annual interest, the person will divide 72 by 8. It will take nine years to double the investment at 8 percent.

When a person borrows money, it is best to find a loan with the lowest interest rate possible. The higher the interest rate, the more money the person will have to pay back. For example, an auto loan of $18,000 with an interest rate of 6.9 percent APR over five years means the person will pay back a total of $24,210. That same loan with an APR of 16.44 percent would cost a total of $32,796.

HIGH-INTEREST DEBT

Loans may be available at low interest rates, but not everyone has access to these rates. Someone who has a bad credit rating—perhaps because the person was late paying bills or attempted to pay bills with no money in his or her account—may not be able to get a

Credit scores affect how much people have to pay each month for their homes and cars.

low-interest loan. To determine whether someone has a good credit rating, the lender requests this person's credit report. The credit report details a person's payment history, how much money the person owes, the length of his or her credit history, how many new credit accounts the person has, and the types of credit he or she has.

The report also gives the person a FICO credit score. Credit scores are like test scores—the higher the number, the better it is. A FICO score of 800 is excellent. This person will have no problem getting a loan. Someone who is late paying bills and writes checks when he or she has no money may have a FICO score of 300, which is very bad. When lenders look at this person's credit history, they will see the person as a bad risk because there is a strong chance he or she will not pay back the loan on time, if at all.

Often, banks won't loan money to people with bad credit, so these people go to payday lenders for loans. The idea behind payday lending is that someone can borrow a relatively small amount of money, such as $500, to help pay emergency expenses. The person will pay the loan back on the next payday, usually in one month or less. Payday lenders may charge extremely high fees and interest rates. For example, a lender might charge a fee of $15 for every $100 borrowed. Someone who borrows $500 would then have

BAD CREDIT

A bad credit history affects more than just loan rates. It can also make it harder for a person to rent an apartment, because the landlord could worry that a tenant with bad credit won't pay the rent. Someone with bad credit may also have more difficulty getting utility services, such as gas, electricity, and water. Utility companies also check a person's credit, and if they see someone has bad credit, these companies often require a deposit, or a sum of money up front. A deposit is paid before service begins so that if the person misses a payment, the utility keeps his or her money.

to pay back a total of $575. This may not sound bad, but it is the equivalent of a loan that charges almost 400 percent APR.[2] Financial experts advise people not to take out payday loans because of these high fees.

COMPOUND INTEREST

It is also important to understand how interest is calculated. These calculations vary depending on whether it is compound interest or simple interest. Simple interest is a set interest rate that is calculated as a percentage of the money lent. If someone takes out a car loan for $18,000 with a simple interest rate of 6.9 percent APR, the person would be charged 6.9 percent of $18,000—or $1,242—for each year of the loan. That means the total interest would be $6,210 for a five-year loan.

Compound interest is calculated not only on the original sum of money but also on the interest that is being added to this total. Because of that, a car loan of $18,000 with a compound APR of 6.9 percent means that for the first year, the total interest is $1,242. For the second year, the interest is charged against the original loan plus the $1,242, so the total interest comes out to $1,327.70. By the end of a five-year car loan, the yearly interest would reach $1,621.93. The total interest would add up to $7,128.18. It is

COMPOUND INTEREST'S PLUS SIDE

Compound interest causes debt to grow, but it does the same thing with investments and savings. Because of this, compound interest on an investment is a very good thing. It enables money left in savings long term to grow rapidly so that investing even small amounts, such as $25 a month, will add up to a significant amount by the time a teen is ready to retire.

important for people to understand how compound interest works so they understand how much they are paying back.

CHANGING RATES

Interest rates aren't static, or unchanging, but rise and fall with changes in the economy. If very few people are trying to take out loans to buy homes, banks drop the interest rates they are charging people to try to get them to take out loans and buy houses. If a lot of people are taking out home loans, but not many people are investing or putting money into savings, banks will raise the interest rates on loans to try to decrease demand. The banks do this because they do not have enough money on hand to meet the demand for loans.

FIXED RATE VS. VARIABLE RATE

A fixed-rate loan is a loan that will have the same interest rate throughout the life of the loan. This means that if interest rates go up or down, the interest rate on the loan remains the same. It can be good to take out a fixed-rate loan when interest rates are climbing, because this locks the loan in at a lower interest rate. The problem is that if someone takes out a large loan, such as a mortgage on a home, and interest rates or home values drop, the person is stuck with a high–interest rate loan. The person will have to pay back more money than if he or she had a lower interest rate.

A variable-rate loan is a loan with an interest rate that will rise and fall with the changing overall rate. If interest rates are dropping, it can be better to take a variable-rate loan so that the rate of the loan drops with the market.

Banks also adjust the interest rates paid on investments. When banks want more people to invest because they are running low on money to loan, they offer higher interest rates on investments. Still, there are limits to how much banks will shift these interest rates.

Banks also borrow from and loan money to each other. The interest rates banks charge each other on these loans are set by the Federal Reserve Bank. The Federal Reserve is the central bank in the United States. These interest rates set by the Federal Reserve influence the rates banks offer their customers.

SIMPLE VS. COMPOUND INTEREST

Calculate the interest for three years as well as the total paid using both simple and compound interest. See just how big the difference is between these two types of interest.

Loan Amount: $10,000

Interest Rate: 6.9% (use .069 in calculations)

Term of Loan: Three years

SIMPLE INTEREST

Simple interest is calculated on the loan amount. For a three-year loan, the interest is calculated for each year. Fill in the blanks below to find the total amount paid back.

Interest Year One

_____ x _____ = _____
Loan amount x interest rate = Interest year one
$10,000   .069 $690

Interest Year Two

_____ x _____ = _____
Loan amount x interest rate = Interest year two
$10,000   .069 $690

Interest Year Three

_____ x _____ = _____
Loan amount x interest rate = Interest year three
$10,000   .069 $690

COMPOUND INTEREST

Compound interest is calculated each year on the loan amount plus the interest from the previous years. Fill in the blanks below to find the total amount paid back.

Interest Year One

_____ x _____ = _____
Loan amount x interest rate = Interest year one
$10,000   .069 $690

Interest Year Two

_____ x _____ = _____
Loan amount x interest rate = Interest year two
+ interest year one
$10,690   .069 $737.61

Interest Year Three

_____ x _____ = _____
Loan amount x interest rate = Interest year three
+ interest year one
+ interest year two
$11,427.61   .069 $788.51

AMOUNT REPAID

To figure out how much is repaid in total, add the interest amounts to the amount of the original loan.

SIMPLE INTEREST	COMPOUND INTEREST
Loan amount _____	Loan amount _____
Interest year one_____	Interest year one _____
Interest year two _____	Interest year two _____
Interest year three _____	Interest year three _____
Total_____	Total _____

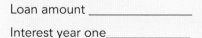

CHAPTER SIX

INVESTING

When someone saves money, the person is putting it aside so he or she will have it later. Savings accounts, checking accounts, and CDs are safe places to put money because they are insured by the Federal Deposit Insurance Corporation, or FDIC. Congress created this agency to keep Americans' finances safe. It does this, in part, by insuring banks and the money these institutions contain. Banks rarely fail. But even if they do, a person with money in the bank will get that money back. Normally, at the end of the savings period, the person will still have his or her savings and some interest. There is very little risk, and it is relatively easy to withdraw this money.

Investments are riskier because the money is not insured by the federal government. There are no guarantees that at the end of several months or several years the person will have any income or even the money that was originally invested, which is called the principal. Despite the risk of loss, a good investment

Stock values change constantly.

will result in more income than the person would have made through savings. Because of this possibility for higher earnings, most people are willing to take a risk.

LIFE INSURANCE

One type of investment is life insurance. Life insurance is a contract between the insurer and the policyholder. The insured person agrees to pay into the fund, and the insurance company agrees to pay this person's family a set amount of money if the person dies. It sounds grim, but life insurance ensures that a person's family can continue to pay bills, buy food, and have somewhere to live if the person who is paying for these things dies. Most teens don't need life insurance since no one is relying on their income, but many parents have it because their children depend on their earnings for living expenses such as food, shelter, and clothing.

The trick with life insurance is deciding how much to get. Some people get a policy that will pay off large expenses, such as their house. Others get a policy that will replace their income for a set number of years. The more the life insurance company pays out as a death benefit, the more the insurance policy costs.

People take out life insurance to protect their loved ones in case something happens to them.

STOCKS

Another form of investment is buying stocks. A company that is looking for people to invest in it offers shares of stock for sale. When investors buy these shares, they then own a small part of the company. A stock sale results in the company having cash to pay employees and make necessary purchases. Later the investors might get dividends—a portion of the company's income. If someone buys 100 shares of stock and the company pays a yearly dividend of $1,

PUBLIC VS. PRIVATE

Companies that publicly trade their stocks offer them for sale through one or more of the major stock exchanges, such as the New York Stock Exchange. To be listed on one of these exchanges, the company must follow strict guidelines set by the Securities and Exchange Commission and other regulatory bodies. These groups make sure the companies that publicly sell stocks meet certain standards to make the stock market fair for all investors. Not all companies publicly trade their stock. Privately owned companies might only sell stocks to their own employees or to a small number of investors.

the person will make $100 that year. A wide variety of companies offer stocks, including computer companies such as HP, retailers such as Target, and hotels such as Marriott International.

People can choose to purchase stocks based on their own study of the market or simply by picking companies they enjoy doing business with. But it is hard for someone who doesn't do this as a business to keep track of the ups and downs of the market and to know which areas of the market are increasing in value and which are decreasing. One common piece of investment advice is to buy low and sell high. This means that people should buy a stock when the price is

BIAS BASICS

People who try to manage their own investments, including stock purchases, often end up reading books and closely watching the news to learn what they need to know to make smart investment decisions. Sources might discuss which businesses are undertaking new ventures that might lead to a rise in their stocks' value. They could also note which companies have a powerful leader stepping down with no replacement in sight, which can cause the company to drop in value as people worry that it might struggle. But books, newsletters, blogs, and podcasts also reflect the biases of their authors, because many people give financial advice based on what will benefit them personally. A broker may advise people to sell one stock and buy another in hopes of getting commissions on both the sale and the purchase. It can be hard to tell who is giving sound advice that doesn't benefit them in some way. Many people who write about the stock market will include a disclaimer about which stocks they own personally. That way, the reader knows how the author might benefit from good or bad news about a particular company.

low and then sell the stock when it is worth much more. Doing this, they will maximize their profits, making the most money possible. But doing this requires knowing stock values and how low or high a certain stock is likely to go. Because of the time-consuming nature of tracking the market, many people invest in mutual funds.

NOW OR LATER?

Use this flowchart to decide whether a short-term or long-term investment is the better immediate choice.

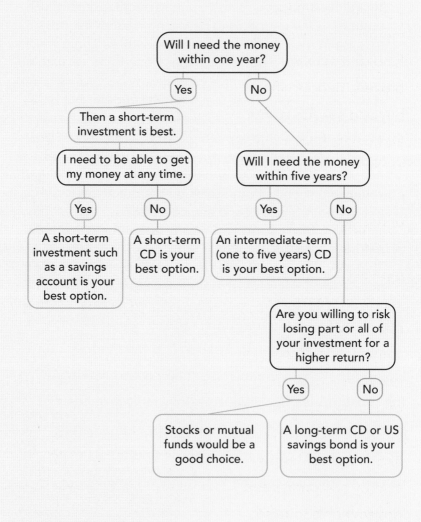

Will I need the money within one year?

Yes → Then a short-term investment is best.

No → Will I need the money within five years?

Then a short-term investment is best.

I need to be able to get my money at any time.

Yes → A short-term investment such as a savings account is your best option.

No → A short-term CD is your best option.

Will I need the money within five years?

Yes → An intermediate-term (one to five years) CD is your best option.

No → Are you willing to risk losing part or all of your investment for a higher return?

Are you willing to risk losing part or all of your investment for a higher return?

Yes → Stocks or mutual funds would be a good choice.

No → A long-term CD or US savings bond is your best option.

MUTUAL FUNDS

One of the safest forms of investment is the mutual fund. Mutual funds are managed by brokers, people who buy and sell the stocks and bonds held in these accounts. These funds combine the money of a large number of investors and use this money to invest in a variety of stocks or bonds, or sometimes a combination of the two. In addition to savings bonds, mutual funds can include corporate bonds and municipal bonds, sold by companies and governments to raise the money needed for various projects.

MUTUALLY EXCLUSIVE

Among the different kinds of mutual funds are stock funds and bond funds. Some stock funds invest in a wide variety of companies, but others narrow their focus. One fund might invest only in US companies, while another might only deal with international companies. Some funds may be limited to certain sectors, such as technology or transportation. Bond funds are primarily organized around how long the bonds take to mature, with each fund focusing on short-term, intermediate-term, or long-term bonds. The bonds are generally a combination of treasury bonds, municipal bonds issued by individual cities, and corporate bonds issued by companies. Sector funds make it possible for someone to invest in one sector of the market, such as health care, technology, or even social media.

Investors in a particular fund do not own the bonds or the stocks. Instead, they own shares in the fund, which, at any time, may sell some of the stocks or bonds it holds while also adding new items.

A mutual fund is a diverse form of investment, which also makes it less risky. The idea is that when one stock does poorly and drops, another might do well and balance out the loss. The diverse array of stocks and bonds in a mutual fund is professionally managed.

With a large number of mutual funds to choose from, investment experts advise would-be investors to research various funds. They should check to see how well these funds have done over time and invest in one that has historically done well. However, past performance is not always an indicator of future performance. People should also be aware that some funds charge ongoing management fees, which can eat into a person's profits.

TRACKING INVESTMENTS

Use this fill-in-the-blank worksheet to track the changing value of stocks. Pick some companies, look up their stock market symbols, and then track those stocks. How much are the stocks worth now? How much are they worth three weeks later?

Name of Stock	Stock Symbol	Price in Week One	Price in Week Three	Gain/Loss

CHAPTER SEVEN

INVESTING AT WORK

L ife insurance, stocks, and funds aren't the only types of investments. There are also a wide variety of investments that some employers make available to their employees. Employer-enabled investments can help employees save enough money to retire or pay for their children's college.

Some young employees put off taking part in these programs, in part because things such as retirement can seem like a long way off to people in their twenties. But people who start adding money to employer-enabled accounts in their twenties can have substantial investment funds by the time they turn 50 years old. As with other forms of investment or savings, a small amount put aside regularly over a long period of time adds up. This is especially true if an employer is willing to match funds in one of several types of accounts that allow employees to invest through work.

Retirement plans such as 401(k)s can be invested in both stocks and bonds. As people get older, they typically want to invest in more bonds because bonds are more secure.

401(k) Plan

ollment Applicat

fore Completing this Form, read the back for important information regarding

Please type or print clearly using Black Ink.

3. Sign the form in the presence of a Notary Public.

nt Information
First Name

ddress (Include Number, Str

ng Address, if different (Include P.O. Box, or General Delivery, City, State, Zip

hone

Code)

5. Former Nam

7. Driver's Li

MATCHING FUNDS

When an employer offers matching funds or matching contributions, it means that when an employee invests $10 for retirement, for example, the employer matches the contribution. Sometimes the match is dollar for dollar, so $10 for $10, and sometimes it is $0.50 on the dollar, so $5 for $10. Some employers put a cap on the amount they will match, contributing up to a certain percentage of the employee's annual income. To take advantage of a matching program, employees must be willing to invest in their own retirement. Yet employees who are willing to make this investment earn the matching funds, receiving a bonus unavailable to people who don't participate. Someone who is planning to look for a new job may not want to take advantage of matching funds. In many companies, these funds are not vested to the employee, becoming his or her property, for another two or three years. If a person leaves before that time, the funds must be returned.

RETIREMENT ACCOUNTS

Retirement is a time when older people quit working. Retirement accounts are accounts that help individuals put aside money for living expenses when they reach the age when they no longer have regular paychecks. Among the most well-known employer-sponsored retirement accounts are 401(k)s, 403(b)s, 457s, and Thrift Savings Plans. With these accounts, the employee decides how much he or she wants to contribute, and the employer, using payroll deduction, puts the money into the appropriate account.

The employer sponsors the program and transfers the money into the account, but it does not manage the actual investments. Instead, another company is hired to do so. Retirement accounts are managed by mutual fund companies, including Fidelity and Vanguard, brokerage firms such as Merrill Lynch, and insurance companies such as Prudential.

A 401(k) is a retirement account used by for-profit companies, or companies that work to make a profit. These are often the same companies that offer stocks. The money that is deposited into a 401(k) is a payroll deduction, often pretax, or happening before tax is paid. These accounts and the income they generate are tax deferred, meaning

PAYROLL DEDUCTIONS

Financial advisers recommend that people who want to build their savings or investments use payroll deduction. By automatically putting money into a savings account, 401(k), or other retirement plan, the employee doesn't even have to think about the account. The only effort required by the investor is to sign up for the program. Once this has been done, the investment is entirely automatic.

the person who owns the account pays neither federal nor state income tax before he or she retires and starts drawing on the account. The taxes must be paid once the person retires and starts to take money out of this account. The amount of money someone can put into a 401(k) is limited by laws put into place by Congress to keep wealthy people from avoiding taxes. In 2019, someone could put $19,000 per year into a 401(k).[1]

A 403(b) works the same way as a 401(k), but it is used by nonprofit organizations such as public schools.

PRETAX INVESTMENTS

The idea behind pretax investment isn't to avoid paying taxes but to delay paying taxes. If people pay taxes first, they have less money left to invest. By deferring, or delaying, taxes, they have a larger sum of money to invest, earning even more interest. Once money is removed from the account, the taxes must be paid on both the funds that were originally invested as well as the earnings.

There are limits to how much money someone can put into these accounts as well, with $19,000 being the maximum in 2019.[2] A 457 is used by people who work for city or state governments, while a Thrift Savings Plan is for employees of the federal government, including members of the military. The limit is the same for a 457 as a 403(b) and a 401(k).

IRAS AND ROTH IRAS

Other retirement options include Individual Retirement Accounts (IRAs) and Roth IRAs. People can contribute to an IRA or Roth IRA whether or not they also have a 401(k), a 403(b), a 457, or a Thrift Savings Plan. IRAs are ideal for people whose employers don't offer retirement accounts or for those who want to invest over and above the amount they can legally put into other retirement accounts.

There are limits to how much can be put into an IRA as well. In 2019, a person could contribute $6,000 annually. However, if the person is 50 years old or older, then the limit is $7,000.[3] Some IRA contributions

PENSIONS

Pensions are employer-funded retirement plans. The money is not taken out of the employee's check or income but is put into the plan by the employer. These plans are not common because they are expensive to maintain. Because of this, they are found at large companies, in government jobs, and in some teaching jobs. People whose benefits include pensions may be vested, or eligible to receive payment, after only five years of employment with the company. No matter when they qualify, they will not receive any payment until after they reach retirement age.

are tax deductible. This means the person who owns the account does not pay taxes on the money that goes into the IRA. Whether contributions are deductible depends on total household earnings and the total amount the person has invested in the IRA. The money placed into an IRA will be taxed when it is withdrawn following retirement.

Someone whose contributions would not be tax free might consider a Roth IRA. While the investment itself is not tax deductible, the earnings are not taxed.

ESOP

Another option for retirement investment is an employee stock ownership program (ESOP). ESOPs are offered by publicly and privately traded companies. Through these programs, employers offer their employees the opportunity to buy a set number of shares per year. Some companies match the employee's investment to encourage saving for retirement. This is a widespread form of investment, with 6,669 programs operating in the United States and approximately 14.4 million US employees taking part.[4]

The idea behind this type of program is to benefit both the company and the employee. The employee

Financial experts say that people should start saving for retirement as soon as they start working.

gets an investment that allows him or her to share company profits. Because the growth of this investment depends on how well the company performs, the employee is that much more interested in seeing the company succeed and will work harder toward that end.

Investment toward a secure retirement can occur in many forms, ranging from employer-provided pensions to IRAs and Roth IRAs that are entirely funded by the individual. These programs help people maximize their investments and put money aside for the future. Just how quickly invested money will grow depends on the risk.

TEST YOUR INVESTMENT KNOWLEDGE

Answer these true/false statements to see how much you know about these investment opportunities.

- Putting money in a tax-deferred investment means the person never pays taxes on this income.
  True or False

- Retirement accounts are accounts that people start putting money into after they retire. True or False

- Employer-enabled accounts are managed by the person's employer. True or False

- An investor can put money into either a 401(k) or an IRA but not both. True or False

- 401(k) accounts are available only to employees of the federal government and active military members.
  True or False

- An investor can only put $5,500 into a 401(k) retirement account. True or False

- All US employees are eligible for pensions.
  True or False

- ESOPs allow employees to put money into bonds.
  True or False

Did you know all of these statements were false? It's important for people to be able to spot inaccurate information that can impact their financial future.

CHAPTER EIGHT

RISK AND RETURNS

T wo common investment terms are *risk* and *returns*. When people invest money, they either make income or lose money. The income and losses are both called returns because they are the return on the investment.

Risk is the chance that a person will lose all or part of an initial investment. Investments that have a low risk—or very little chance that someone will lose his or her principal—offer less income. A person who saves money or invests in something that is low risk will end up with his or her principal and a little more.

Investments with a high level of risk or uncertainty can offer a high level of return. The person who makes a high-risk investment may lose all or part of the principal, or he or she may make only a small return. But there is also the chance that the person will make a great deal compared to the original investment. These investments are risky, but when they are

People should be aware of the trade-off between risk and return for their investments.

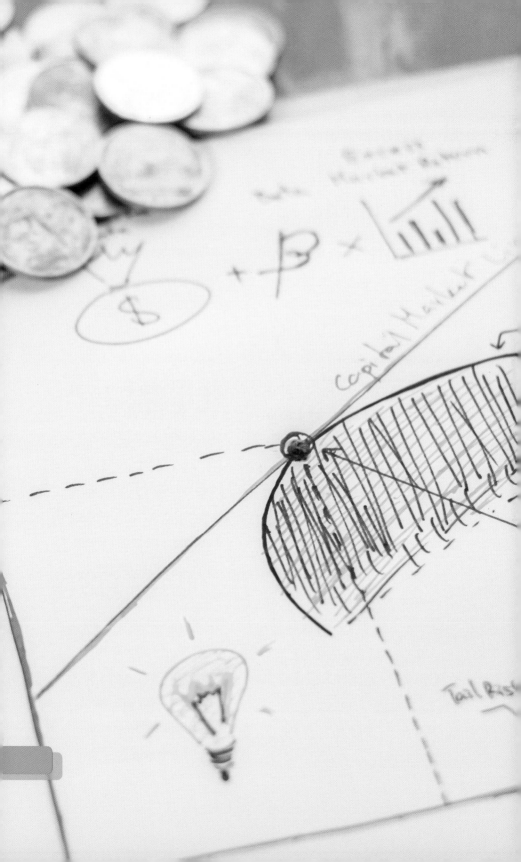

THE STOCK MARKET CRASH AND THE GREAT DEPRESSION

A stock market crash is a rapid drop in stock prices. The people who own these stocks lose a lot of money. Concerned stockholders can cause a crash. If a sudden event occurs, such as a natural disaster, and people begin to panic, they will try to sell their stocks to avoid losing the money they had invested. The US stock market crashed in 1929. Some financial experts believe this happened because stocks had been overpriced, selling for more than they were worth. People borrowed money to buy these stocks. When the inflated prices dropped, people were left owing much more than the stocks were then worth. This was one of the causes of the Great Depression, a severe economic downturn that lasted throughout the 1930s.

successful, the payoff is high. However, not everyone is comfortable risking money in this way. Some people are generally happier making low-risk investments. How much risk a person is willing to take is called risk-tolerance level.

LOW RISK

No one likes to lose money, especially money that they were planning to use to buy a house, pay off their car, or go to college. For people who aren't comfortable with the possibility of losing their money, low-risk investments are best. Certain accounts are low risk because, since 1933, they have been insured by the federal government. The money in these accounts is safe. Even if the bank fails, the insurance will give the investor back at least the principal.

Some forms of low-risk savings and investment include credit card rewards, such as a credit card that offers cash back bonuses based on the amount of money a person spent. Another form of low-risk investment is stocks that pay dividends. These stocks are generally available from stable companies, and investors can expect at least some profit. Money market funds combine CDs and bonds with other low-risk investments, and people buy shares of the fund.

These types of investments don't offer the opportunity for immense profit, but they are safe. Low-risk investments are especially good for people who will need the money soon.

HIGH RISK

Not everyone is willing to risk their principal, but for people who are, the payoffs can be immense. High-risk investments are, as the term implies, risky. Not only might there be no income but the investor may lose the principal that he or she put into the investment.

Although stocks that pay dividends from established companies are considered low risk, this is not the case for all stocks. An initial public offering is when a company first makes its stock available for purchase. Newer companies don't have a track record, so no one knows whether the companies are going to succeed or fail. Some people who get in early on such companies make a massive amount of money when the companies turn out to be wildly successful. However, there are many companies that make initial public offerings but then fail. The people who invested in the companies' stocks lose their money. Venture capitalists also put money into new companies.

Other high-risk investments include new foreign companies and high-yield bonds from foreign countries.

VENTURE CAPITAL

Venture capital is the money, or capital, that helps a new business venture take off. Venture capitalists, people who specialize in this type of investment, focus on different aspects ranging from helping a company get started to helping it grow. The ultimate goal of many venture capitalists is to make the company large and successful enough that a larger company will want to buy it out. This can result in huge profits for early investors.

Chris Sacca is one venture capitalist who invested in Twitter.

If a country undergoes major industrial growth, people will be selling stocks for its new and growing companies. Governments will also be selling bonds to improve their highways, airports, and other services to make their country more attractive to travelers and investors. To get people to invest, these companies and governments have to promise larger profits. That's because the risk is very real that a company or government in an unstable area may fail to thrive or a government may be overthrown altogether.

DIVERSIFICATION

Financial experts advise investors to diversify their holdings, or spread their investments out into several different areas. This means they shouldn't have only high-risk investments, only low-risk investments, or only one type of investment, such as stocks in a single company or life insurance.

A person whose entire investment portfolio consists of investments in a single company depends on that company doing well. But if there is an industry downturn—such as what happened in the US automotive industry from 2008 to 2010—someone who has invested in only one company will be in trouble

In 2008, large automotive companies were struggling financially. General Motors and Chrysler filed for bankruptcy, and the US government bailed them out.

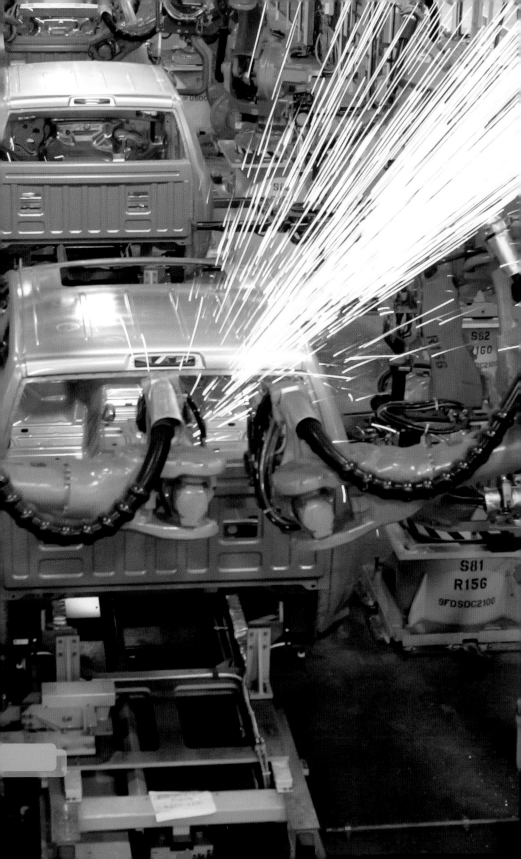

TIME MATTERS

When people discuss investments and stocks, some of them talk about when to buy and when to sell. Often when the value of a stock starts to drop, they panic and sell. Instead of doing this, financial advisers recommend that people separate their emotions from their investment strategy. Although their portfolio will require minor adjustments from time to time, investors need to remember that building their portfolio's value takes time. Trying to time the market is needlessly stressful because the market changes constantly and is difficult to predict. Instead, they should let their investments ride. Discipline in actually making investments and patience in giving things time to recover from a drop and to continue building are the key to a successful investment strategy. Colton Dillion of the Acorn investment app offers this advice: "Investors who start early, practice patience and stick to a long-term investing strategy often see the best returns and financial success."[1]

financially. If this person had invested in stocks from various companies, the portfolio as a whole would be in better shape. In addition to multiple types of stock, people should go beyond stocks and have CDs and bonds. If they have enough money that they can afford to lose some of it, they could also buy into a high-risk investment, such as an overseas company or bond.

CALCULATING OR IDENTIFYING RISK

Just how risky is a particular stock? Stock analysts determine this by calculating the stock's beta. Beta is a measurement of one stock's risk compared to the market as a whole.

Overall, the stock market has a beta of one, because it is the baseline against which single stocks are measured. When a stock has a beta of one, the price can vary as much as the general market. If a stock has a beta of higher than one, it is riskier than the market as a whole, while a beta of lower than one is less risky. Pick five companies and find their beta. Then, determine whether the stock is risky.

Name of Stock	Stock Symbol	Beta	Risky? Yes or No

CHAPTER NINE

SETTING GOALS AND PLANNING FOR THE FUTURE

A s with any habit, whether it's exercise or turning off the lights, good money habits don't just happen. And teens should start developing good money habits as soon as possible. Katy Osborn, a reporter for *Money* magazine, suggests that teens start with how they see themselves. Instead of thinking of themselves as people who wear the latest fashions or have the latest technology, teens could view themselves as people who know how to get a good deal on what they want and still have money in the bank.

Teens should save up and think about purchases before they make them.

GOOD HEALTH

Most people realize exercise and a good diet can help them stay healthy and live longer, but what they may not realize is that being healthy can actually save money. Home-cooked meals are healthier than eating out, so someone who cooks at home can save money and help maintain his or her health. In a study published in 2012, Cleveland State University professor Vasilios Kosteas reports that people who exercise at least three times a week even earn 6 to 9 percent more than those who don't.[1] This is perhaps because exercise helps them handle stress better and stay more alert.

SAVING FOR FUTURE GOALS

It's important for teens to think about and plan to put money aside for future goals. How much people need to have saved at any time depends on where they are in life and what their plans are. If someone wants to buy a house, he should save enough money to have a down payment that won't wipe out his savings. To begin, a person should look at housing costs in the area where she wants to live and then calculate 20 percent of the value of the home. A down payment of less than 20 percent requires that the buyer have

Teenagers can put money aside to pay for college, and they should check their bank accounts regularly.

619.80

9.80

.30

.30

28447.30

24031.30

24926.67

24926.72

TECHNOLOGY MATTERS

To help develop good savings habits, experts suggest that teens make use of technology that can help them put money aside. The reality is that there are times when people won't think about saving because they are busy with other things. By using automated savings, money will be put aside regularly. One trick is to have paychecks direct deposited into two accounts. Ninety percent of each check goes into an account to pay expenses. Ten percent goes into a separate savings account that is not accessed and is allowed to gather interest over the long term. In addition, there are apps, such as Acorn, that automate small investments. Acorn connects to the user's bank account and, when bills are paid, rounds all payments up to the nearest dollar and invests the excess in index funds, a type of combined stock or bond fund. Technology can take care of savings when people are living busy lives.

mortgage insurance, which can cost as much as 0.5 to 1 percent of the total house loan.[2] It may not seem like much money, but it adds to the cost of the loan. Investments can help people save for big expenses such as a house. Smaller expenses may not require investments, but it could still take several months or a year to save the money needed to cover certain expenses, such as the cost of a trip.

Taking trips overseas to visit family or friends can be expensive, so it's smart to budget for them.

Experts advise people to keep a certain amount of money as emergency savings, or savings that will pay all of their expenses if they lose their job. The smallest recommended amount is enough to pay their living expenses for three months. This amount is acceptable for someone who has a reliable job and family or friends who might be able to help out in an emergency.

Someone who has a job with highly fluctuating income, like a writer, real estate agent, or salesperson working solely for commission, should save enough to meet expenses for a full year. Because these people don't know how much they will make from year to year, it is better for

DEBT-TO-INCOME RATIO

Debt-to-income ratio is the relationship between a person's debt and her income. Someone who makes a monthly house payment of $1,200 and pays off approximately $800 in credit card bills monthly but has no other expenses has $2,000 in monthly debt. If her monthly income is $6,000, her debt-to-income ratio would be figured out by dividing debt ($2,000) by income ($6,000). That comes out to 33.33 percent. Someone with monthly expenses of $4,000 and an income of $6,000 has a debt-to-income ratio of 66.66 percent. A lower percentage is better because it shows that the person has low debt compared to her income.

COLLEGE COSTS (2018-2019)[3]

A college education is one expense that many people go into debt for.

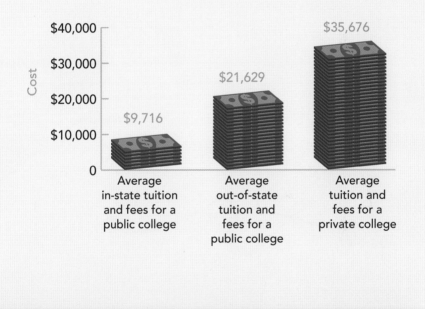

them to have a large amount of money put aside. Since their income fluctuates so much, they are more likely to have trouble meeting expenses, and this money may come in handy.

DEBT ISN'T ENTIRELY AVOIDABLE

For most people, debt isn't entirely avoidable because certain things cost a lot of money. Very few people are going to wait to go to college, buy a house, or buy a car until they have saved all of the money needed to pay for these expenses up front.

When people know how much money they are earning, as well as how much they are probably going to earn in the near future, they can estimate what they can afford to spend now. They can keep some debt, such as credit card debt, manageable by paying it off monthly, which limits how much debt accumulates. By making a habit of keeping the amount they owe low, people can take on other debt with reasonable confidence that they will be able to pay it off.

It also helps to understand good debt versus bad debt. Good debt is borrowing money for something that will increase in value and help earn more money later on. Bad debt is borrowing money at a high interest rate. It is also borrowing more than something is worth or more than can be repaid. High-interest

People view mortgages as a type of good debt.

student loans are bad debt. Putting an expensive vacation on a credit card is also bad debt.

SECURITY

Experts warn young adults in college to protect their personal information because they are prime targets for identity theft. Thieves gather students' data when students use unsecured networks or walk away from their laptops. Once the thieves have a student's Social Security number and name, they can file for a student's tax return to get the student's money. Thieves can also get credit cards in a student's name, leaving the young adult to pay the bill. Young adults can stay safe by guarding all paperwork with their Social Security number, logging out of accounts, and using passwords or thumbprints to protect all of their devices.

If people plan what they want now and in the future, they will have a better idea how much they can spend and what they want to spend it on. Someone who wants to buy a house may not want to buy an expensive car or go on an international vacation at the same time. Someone who wants a vacation may choose to live in an apartment instead of buying a house. Sometimes people have to make trade-offs, deciding what things are priorities and doing without other things.

Having large amounts of debt can be stressful. Budgeting for expenses can help people avoid debt.

Planning savings as well as planning where and how much to spend will give people a good debt-to-income ratio and help keep their debt manageable.

Learning about money isn't a skill that only teenagers need. Once people learn to track their income and put money into savings and investments, they can start to build a secure financial future for themselves. When their circumstances change, such as when they get a better job or decide to pursue higher education, they can reevaluate their situation. They have the knowledge they will need to plan out their financial future.

EMERGENCY SAVINGS

How much money do you need to put aside in case of an emergency? Answer these questions to help you decide.

1. My income is:

   a. Reliable
   b. Fluctuates wildly

2. I have family members I can rely on for financial help.

   a. Yes
   b. No

3. My expenses:

   a. Are consistent month to month.
   b. Vary greatly from one month to the next.

If you answered "a" more often than you answered "b," you can probably put aside enough money to meet your expenses for three months. If you answered "b" more often than "a," you should put aside enough to pay your expenses for one year. If you aren't sure how much money you spend in three months or in one year, track your earnings and your spending.

KEY TAKEAWAYS

TOP 10 MOST IMPORTANT CONCEPTS

1. Financial security takes planning.

2. A job is more than income. Benefits and potential job expenses should also be considered.

3. Take-home pay is what is left in a paycheck after taxes and other deductions are made.

4. People don't have to spend discretionary income.

5. Savings bonds and CDs can be used to put money aside for college.

6. Investing can help people make money.

7. Someone with a low risk tolerance should stick with low-risk savings and investments.

8. Budgets and financial plans should be regularly reviewed and updated.

9. Diverse investments and patience are key to making money through investments.

10. Saving money is a habit that takes time to form.

TOP 5 TAHEAWAYS

1. Start saving today for big purchases.

2. Open a bank account. Put savings in the bank where they can earn interest.

3. Make a budget. A budget shows not only how much money is coming in but where it is being spent.

4. Gather job application information and figure out what type of job could support your lifestyle.

5. Set a goal for emergency saving. Decide how much money you need to set aside for an emergency.

GLOSSARY

annual percentage rate (APR)
Interest, calculated annually, that is charged on a loan or earned on an investment.

credit history
A person's history of paying bills.

credit union
A financial organization that gives members low interest rates on small loans while also offering accounts such as checking and savings.

earnings
Income; possibly the income on an investment or savings.

inflation
An increase in the price of goods and services over time.

insured
To have paid for coverage in case of a loss, such as that from fire or flooding. The coverage gives people money to help replace what was damaged or destroyed.

interest
A fee charged when a person or business borrows money, or money paid to people as an incentive for keeping their money in a bank.

investors
People who put money into businesses with the hopes of making more money.

mutual fund
A fund that invests in a combination of stocks and bonds and that is managed by brokers.

promissory
Making a promise.

return
Income or loss on an investment.

stock
A piece of ownership in a company. When a person buys "stock," he or she buys a little piece (called a "share") of ownership in a company.

ADDITIONAL RESOURCES

SELECTED BIBLIOGRAPHY

Carlozo, Lou. "10 Long-Term Investing Strategies that Work." *US News & World Report*, 3 May 2018, money.usnews.com. Accessed 20 Sept. 2018.

Olen, Helaine. *The Index Card: Why Personal Finance Doesn't Have to be Complicated.* Portfolio/Penguin, 2016.

"The Rule of 72." *Oklahoma State Department of Education*, n.d., sde.ok.gov. Accessed 20 Sept. 2018.

FURTHER READINGS

Butler, Tamsen. *The Complete Guide to Personal Finance for Teenagers and College Students.* Atlantic, 2016.

Donohue, Moira. *Making Smart Money Choices.* Abdo, 2020.

ONLINE RESOURCES

 Booklinks
NONFICTION NETWORK
FREE! ONLINE NONFICTION RESOURCES

To learn more about earning, saving, and investing, please visit **abdobooklinks.com** or scan this QR code. These links are routinely monitored and updated to provide the most current information available.

MORE INFORMATION

For more information on this subject, contact or visit the following organizations:

FEDERAL RESERVE BANK OF SAINT LOUIS
One Federal Reserve Bank Plaza
Broadway and Locust Streets
Saint Louis, MO 63102
1-800-333-0810
stlouisfed.org
The Federal Reserve Bank of Saint Louis provides videos and exercises to make it easy to learn about economics and financial literacy.

MAPPING YOUR FUTURE
PO Box 2578
Sugar Land, TX 77487-2578
800-374-4072
mappingyourfuture.org
This nonprofit organization focuses on helping students and their parents with the student loan process.

SOURCE NOTES

CHAPTER 1. MONEY MATTERS

None.

CHAPTER 2. GETTING A JOB

1. Susan Johnston Taylor. "5 Ways to Spend Gift Cards Wisely."
   US News, 27 Dec. 2011, money.usnews.com. Accessed
   30 Nov. 2018.

2. Emily Canal. "How This 16-Year-Old Founder Built a $600,000
   Bow Tie Business." *Inc.*, n.d., inc.com. Accessed 30 Nov. 2018.

CHAPTER 3. TAKE-HOME PAY

1. Karina Shedrofsky. "Where Does All Your Money Go?
   Your Paycheck Explained." *USA Today*, 31 Oct. 2016,
   usatoday.com. Accessed 30 Nov. 2018.

2. "Fact Sheet Social Security." *Social Security Administration*,
   n.d., ssa.gov. Accessed 30 Nov. 2018.

3. "What Is Social Security?" *National Academy of Social
   Insurance*, n.d., nasi.org. Accessed 30 Nov. 2018.

4. "What Is Social Security?"

5. "How Much Do You Have to Make to File Taxes—What
   Is the Minimum Income to File Taxes?" *H&R Block*, n.d.,
   hrblock.com. Accessed 30 Nov. 2018.

CHAPTER 4. WAYS TO SAVE

1. Marisa Torrieri. "Are You Paying Yourself First? The Money Habit That Can Boost Wealth." *Forbes*, 24 July 2014, forbes.com. Accessed 30 Nov. 2018.

2. Taylor Tepper. "Despite an Improving Economy, 20% of Americans Aren't Saving Any Money." *Bankrate*, 14 Mar. 2018, bankrate.com. Accessed 30 Nov. 2018.

3. "Best Online Savings Accounts." *Bankrate*, n.d., bankrate.com. Accessed 30 Nov. 2018.

4. Spencer Tierney. "How Much Do the Best CDs Earn?" *Nerd Wallet*, 2 Nov. 2018, nerdwallet.com. Accessed 30 Nov. 2018.

CHAPTER 5. INTEREST

1. "Average Auto Loan Interest Rates: 2018 Facts & Figures." *ValuePenguin*, n.d., valuepenguin.com. Accessed 30 Nov. 2018.

2. "What Is a Payday Loan?" *Consumer Financial Protection Bureau*, 2 June 2017, consumerfinance.gov. Accessed 30 Nov. 2018.

CHAPTER 6. INVESTING

None.

SOURCE NOTES CONTINUED

CHAPTER 7. INVESTING AT WORK

1. Emily Brandon. "New 401(k) and IRA Limits for 2019." *US News*, 12 Nov. 2018, money.usnews.com. Accessed 30 Nov. 2018.

2. Brandon, "New 401(k) and IRA Limits for 2019."

3. Brandon, "New 401(k) and IRA Limits for 2019."

4. Catherine Schnaubelt. "When to Consider an Employee Stock Ownership Plan." *Forbes*, 23 Aug. 2018, forbes.com. Accessed 30 Nov. 2018.

CHAPTER 8. RISK AND RETURNS

1. Lou Carlozo. "Long-Term Investing Strategies That Work." *US News*, 17 Dec. 2015, money.usnews.com. Accessed 30 Nov. 2018.

CHAPTER 9. SETTING GOALS AND PLANNING FOR THE FUTURE

1. Susie Poppick. "10 Things to Know about Money before You're 20." *Time*, 25 Sept. 2015, time.com. Accessed 30 Nov. 2018.

2. "6 Reasons to Avoid Private Mortgage Insurance." *Investopedia*, n.d., investopedia.com. Accessed 30 Nov. 2018.

3. Farran Powell. "See the Average Costs of Attending College in 2018–2019." *US News*, 10 Sept. 2018, usnews.com. Accessed 30 Nov. 2018.

INDEX

INDEX CONTINUED

ABOUT THE AUTHOR

Sue Bradford Edwards is a Missouri nonfiction author who writes about science, the social sciences, and culture. She has written 15 other books for Abdo Publishing, including *The Evolution of Mammals*, *The Evolution of Reptiles*, and *Hidden Human Computers*.

ABOUT THE CONSULTANT

Dr. Linda Simpson, PhD, CFCS, CPFFE, has been a faculty member in the School of Family and Consumer Sciences at Eastern Illinois University since 1997. She has been the founder and executive director of the Literacy in Financial Education (LIFE) Center. The purpose of the center is to prepare college students to play an active role in managing their personal finances and make informed decisions about saving, spending, and borrowing. Based on the educational programs developed for the center, Dr. Simpson received the 2016 Family Economics and Resource Management Community Award from the Community of Family Economics and Resource Management of the American Association of Family and Consumer Sciences.

Dr. Simpson received a PhD from the University of Illinois and MS and BS degrees from Eastern Illinois University. She has numerous publications and has presented at conferences on the topics of online teaching and learning, budgeting and debt management, and consumer behavior.